Understanding Body Language
in a week

GEOFF RIBBENS
RICHARD THOMPSON

Hodder & Stoughton

A MEMBER OF THE HODDER HEADLINE GROUP

the Institute of Management

The Institute of Management (IM) is the leading
organisation for professional management. Its purpose is
to promote the art and science of management in every
sector and at every level, through research, education,
training and development, and representation of
members' views on management issues.

This series is commissioned by IM Enterprises Limited,
a subsidiary of the Institute of Management, providing
commercial services.

Management House,
Cottingham Road,
Corby,
Northants NN17 1TT
Tel: 01536 204222;
Fax: 01536 201651
Website: http://www.inst-mgt.org.uk

Registered in England no 3834492
Registered office: 2 Savoy Court, Strand,
London WC2R 0EZ

Orders: please contact Bookpoint Ltd, 130 Milton Park, Abingdon, Oxon
OX14 4SB.
Telephone: (44) 01235 400414, Fax: (44) 01235 400454. Lines are open from
9.00–6.00, Monday to Saturday, with a 24 hour message answering service.
Email address: orders@bookpoint.co.uk

British Library Cataloguing in Publication Data
A catalogue record for this title is available from The British Library

ISBN 0 340 78176 9

First published   2000
Impression number   10 9 8 7 6 5 4 3 2
Year   2005 2004 2003 2002 2001

Typeset by Fakenham Photosetting Limited, Fakenham, Norfolk.
Printed in Great Britain for Hodder & Stoughton Educational, a division of
Hodder Headline Plc, 338 Euston Road, London NW1 3BH by Cox & Wyman,
Reading, Berks.

C O N T E N T S

Body language means more than simply physical posture. Posture and gesture tell you a lot, but so do less obvious mannerisms, such as eye contact, speed and tone of voice, facial expressions, and even non-verbal sounds like sighs.

> We believe that understanding body language in the course of our working lives can help us get on, not just because we may look the part, exude confidence and act assertively, but because we can **look beyond what people say to what they really mean**.

Though we may not be aware of it, body language is taught to us from the time that we are born and we spend years developing skills that enable us to interpret other peoples' **intentions, meanings** and **motives**. Most of us take this learning process for granted, so we tend to forget that much of what happens interpersonally actually takes place at this **semi-conscious level**.

By the end of the week we hope to have convinced you that you can:

- carry greater influence
- develop effective powers of persuasion
- improve interpersonal skills
- make more effective presentations
- sell more
- be more assertive and learn how to control others
- reduce negativity and conflict
- spot hidden agendas in conversation
- enhance your career prospects.

Body language?

Managing without words

Would it surprise you to learn that **less than 10%** of the messages we communicate face to face occur through the words we use? If we told you that **tone of voice** accounts for nearly **40%** and **posture and gesture 50%,** would you believe us? Well, according to the findings of research into body language it is true. How can that be possible, you may be asking yourself.

The point is that language is concerned with the expression of thoughts, ideas and feelings and its function is to enable communication to take place. **It doesn't have to be in the form of words** providing that we understand the message and grasp the meaning of what is being conveyed.

Body language does precisely this. By means of non-verbal communication we can convey what we think, how we feel and what we want. But how is this done? Simple. By means of physical posture, gestures, facial expression, tone and strength of voice, and non-verbal sounds. Because we subconsciously use this language in our dealings with others we tend to take it for granted.

Let us imagine communication without body language. When we write we use 'commas', 'full stops', 'exclamation marks' and 'question marks' to illustrate to the reader the pauses in our speech and the tone etc. **If we write with no punctuation it is the same as talking without body language**. If we talk without body language the whole meaning and emphasis of what we say is lost.

We found this example recently:

> Dear John I want a man who knows what love is all about you are generous kind thoughtful people who are not like you admit to being useless and inferior you have ruined me for other men I yearn for you I have no feelings whatsoever when we're apart I can be forever happy will you let me be yours Gloria
>
> If we now add punctuation, we can make the statement meaningful; however the meaning all depends on where you pause and where you add emphasis.
>
> Dear John,
> I want a man who knows what love is all about. You are generous, kind, thoughtful. People who are not like you admit to being useless and inferior. You have ruined me for other men. I yearn for you. I have no feelings whatsoever when we're apart. I can be forever happy. Will you let me be yours?
> Gloria
>
> On the other hand if the emphasis is different, we have:
>
> Dear John,
> I want a man who knows what love is. All about you are generous, kind, thoughtful people, who are not like you. Admit to being useless and inferior. You have ruined me. For other men, I yearn. For you, I have no feelings whatsoever. When we're apart, I can be forever happy. Will you let me be?
>
> Yours, Gloria

Posture congruence

Unconscious mimicry

As work on body language progressed it was found that
people **copied** each other's behaviour without realising,
sometimes to their advantage, sometimes to their distinct
disadvantage.

> In the interview situation, for example, it was observed
> that interviewees responded more positively to
> questions when interviewers practiced **posture
> congruence.** This is where **body position** and **hand
> movements** are in **harmony** between speaker and
> listener, suggesting that they are getting on with each
> other.

Mimicry is, in fact, an indirect way of confirming one's
common ground with the person you are assessing or
trying to convince. In the sales situation, being aware of the
customer's body language and reflecting it in your own can
be positively advantageous providing that you don't go
over the top.

Refinement of ideas such as these throughout the seventies and eighties helped to identify a whole range of attitudes and feelings depicted in posture alone. Determination, attentiveness, curiosity, puzzlement, aloofness, indifference, rejection and self-satisfaction were just some of the more obvious. Even psychiatrists began to realise that they could use their patients' gestures and body postures to evaluate their **'true' feelings** and **'real' concerns**.

Low profile, high gain

The importance of body language can be seen in the sales situation where sales staff who deliberately avoid the appearance of being the dominant player tend to get the best results.

What this means is that a successful sales pitch depends on staying cool, giving the customer **space**, using **open, friendly gestures** and maintaining – literally – a **low profile**. Those who appeared too **defensive** or too **aloof**, on the other hand – particularly on the customer's territory – never got a look in.

What research into body language has proved is that effective management stems from more than just knowledge and words. If these factors were the only important ones, we would probably just send notes to each other. But as most of us know, face-to-face interaction is often the most crucial factor in successfully concluding business, whether it be signing a deal or assessing someone's suitability as a colleague.

You may well be able to gauge an individual's experience and qualifications from a CV, but you will sum up his or her potential, honesty, confidence and abilities in face-to-face contact. This is because observing body language tells you the things that people cannot, will not, or do not wish to say in words. This is why we still value the face-to-face interview.

Intuition

There are, however, certain traps in interpreting another person's body language.

What we sometimes put down to '**intuition**' might well be a combination of things that we have '**sensed**', in other words feelings that we have at a subconscious level. When it comes to knowing how other people function, 'intuition' could be described as a mixture of unrecognised, non-verbal messages about people and situations, which are constantly being updated by experience.

In the selection interview, for example, we often hear people say 'I felt there was something odd about him', or 'I should have trusted my intuition'. The trouble with relying upon intuition is that we don't always know whether we have sufficient grounds for judging someone, or even whether intuition simply reflects one's personal prejudices.

For this reason, we need to be cautious about interpreting non-verbal communication and just think of it as supplying us with strong **clues**. After all, posture, gesture and intonation are subtle and do not, as such, constitute evidence or proof of a way someone thinks or feels. In addition, it is seldom one gesture or posture, but a **combination** of body signals that convey the clues. It is also important to put the body language **in context**: for instance, people may rub their hands together because it is cold, not because they are thinking about money.

Seeing is believing

The manager learning to give presentations may have numerous audiovisual aids at his or her disposal, but the presentation may flop if the individual fails to recognise that he or she is the most important audiovisual aid on the stage. Good presenters need only two things apart from an audience: to be **seen** and to be **heard.**

The more complete the picture of peoples' non-verbal ways of communicating, the more likely it is that you will:

- understand their motives and feelings
- communicate with them more effectively
- establish a rapport with them more readily
- persuade them without undue opposition.

Body words

Sometimes, the expressions that people use – yes, the words they actually speak – to describe certain feelings, provide evidence of the **close relationship** between **spoken language** and **body language**. 'Down in the mouth', 'laid

The most important visual aid is you

back', 'spitting blood', 'walking tall', all suggest **postures** or **gestures** that represent states of mind.

Because we are rarely aware of these connections we fail to take full advantage of them. We will be referring to the significance of body **words** as we go along.

Look into my eyes

Eye contact is a fundamental part of getting on with people and gaining their trust. When it is lacking, communication becomes uncomfortable and it is easy to get the wrong impression of what is going on. There's nothing worse than putting on a great show when the parties involved can't be bothered to look at you, or stare with glazed expressions at the wall behind your head.

The **gaze**, as distinct from the casual glance, tends to convey an interest or intent that has the effect of increasing the other person's awareness of you.

Eye contact also regulates the flow of communication. Briefly holding a look for a few seconds indicates our awareness of what is being said and a readiness to communicate further – rather along the lines of 'I have finished with that, now I can respond to you on my terms'. Waiters and waitresses in restaurants often use a similar technique of avoiding eye contact with their customers until it suits them to do so, thereby giving the clear message: 'I'm too busy to deal with you at the moment.' When they finally do look at you directly, you know that you are about to be attended to.

Studies have found that we maintain eye contact with people 40% of the time when we are talking to them, yet 75% of the time when they are talking to us. As listeners it is important for us to show that we are being attentive to what is being said.

But there is another reason for maintaining eye contact, which has more to do with personal reassurance than respect – it is to determine how sincere the speaker is. What we are doing is summing up how we feel about them by watching their body language and the clues they give about themselves as they perform for us.

One of the first things that managers are told when giving presentations is to maintain eye contact with the audience and not to let their eyes wander. If the presenter looks at

I am too busy to deal with you

the screen or flip chart for too long then rapport with the audience is lost and the presentation is considerably weakened.

Communicators who stick to this simple rule are likely to be seen as more persuasive, truthful, sincere, credible, skilled, informed, experienced, honest and friendly. However unjust it may seem, the confident manager with little knowledge can often out-perform the shy but well-informed manager who fails to maintain eye contact with the audience.

The mark of the confident presenter is to maintain eye contact with the audience in a random fashion, while keeping them all on their toes. There are always pitfalls, even for the best presenters. We tend to look more at those we like and, if we spot a friendly face or an ally in the audience, we will tend to direct our attention to them and neglect the rest of the audience. Then we will have inadvertently lost most of the listeners.

NLP and the mind's eye

In recent years, a body of research, **Neuro-Linguistic Programming**, or **NLP** for short, has suggested that we 'think' in terms of our senses, meaning that the information we draw from the world around us is represented in our minds in the form of pictures, sounds, feelings, smells and tastes.

Each one of us has preferences for 'thinking' in certain ways, at certain times, and therefore differs in the ways we perceive and respond to the world around us. The names given to each of the senses are:

- Visual – thinking in pictures
- Auditory – thinking in sounds
- Kinesthetic – thinking in feelings
- Olfactory – thinking in terms of smell
- Gustatory – thinking in terms of taste

Depending on which part of the world we come from, cultural differences influence the manner in which people think. For example, in the West we are said to 'think' primarily in terms of pictures, sounds and feelings, whereas in the East they think in terms of smell and taste as well.

It has been suggested that for Westerners smell and taste act as 'triggers' to the primary senses of seeing, hearing and feeling. Examples of this are where the smell of food in an unexpected place stimulates the mind's picture of the place you most enjoy going out to dinner, or where the salty taste of sea spray brings back a feeling from a memorable holiday.

Roughly 45% of the population are thought to have a primary preference for thinking in terms of feelings (kinesthetic), compared with 35% in terms of visual images and 20% in auditory form.

What is interesting about these **systems of thinking** is that they influence both the **choice of words** we use in communicating with others, and the **body language** we exhibit. Eyes are especially indicative of what we are thinking, but it is the direction in which they move that tells us whether someone is thinking in terms of pictures, sounds or feelings. For example:

- If we visualise something from past experience our eyes tend to move up and to our left.
- If we are trying to construct a picture from words (to imagine something) our eyes move up and to our right.
- If we are remembering sounds our eyes move across to our left, although if we are *constructing* sounds they move to our right.
- If we are trying to access feelings our eyes move to the right and down.
- If we are talking to ourselves our eyes move to the left and down.
- If we de-focus and stare straight ahead, we are thought to be visualising; that is, thinking more deeply about the picture in our head.

It is possible that looking at the direction of people's eyes could be used by managers in the interview process, but the method is not yet foolproof. For a start, you need to know if the interviewee is left- or right-handed and, given that most people feel uncomfortable when eye contact is maintained for longer than expected, you might make them feel uncomfortable.

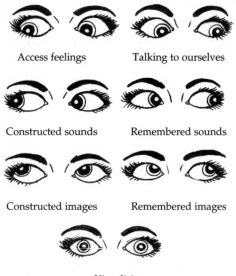

Access feelings   Talking to ourselves

Constructed sounds   Remembered sounds

Constructed images   Remembered images

Visualising

Body thinking

The point about all of this is that if thinking processes are reflected in the way we use our eyes, they probably manifest themselves in other forms of body language as well. 'As the body and mind are inseparable,' write O'Connor and Seymour, 'how we think always shows somewhere, if you know where to look. In particular, it shows in breathing patterns, skin colour and posture.'

And if the mind–body link is true, managers, for example, could benefit from knowing how eye movements convey different kinds of thought processes, thereby enhancing their interpersonal skills.

But what evidence is there to back up such a claim? The same authors have come up with the following examples:

Thinking in visual images
When people do this they tend to speak more quickly and at a higher pitch. In addition, their breathing may be higher in the chest and more shallow. There is often an increase in muscle tension, particularly in the shoulders, the head will be up and the face will often appear paler than normal.

Thinking in sounds
In this case, people tend to breathe evenly over the whole chest area. Small rhythmic movements of the body are discernible and voice tonality is clear, expressive and resonant.The head is well balanced on the shoulders, or held slightly at an angle, as if listening to something.

Talking to oneself
When people do this they often lean their heads to one side, nestling it on their hand or fist. This is known as the 'telephone position', as one gets the impression that they are talking on an invisible telephone. They may actually repeat out loud what they have just 'heard', with the result that you can see their lips move.

Thinking about feelings
This is characterised by deep breathing low in the stomach area. The voice has a deeper tonality to it and the individual will typically speak slowly using long pauses. The body language implicit in Rodin's famous sculpture of The Thinker could be said to suggest kinesthetic thinking.

It has also been observed that when we are involved in different kinds of thinking processes we often gesture towards the sense organ related to it. For example, some people gesture in the direction of their ears while 'listening' to sound cues; others may point to their eyes when 'visualising'. If we 'feel' things particularly strongly we sometimes gesture towards the abdomen.

Although these examples indicate how people think in relation to how they act, they do not necessarily tell us what they are thinking. For counsellors and selection interviewers, whose job it is to interpret what they hear, such techniques could nevertheless provide **valuable clues**.

Getting it together

If people think in terms of pictures, sounds and feelings, then how do we know if two people are 'thinking' along the same lines? For example, if we are talking together in coaching, training, sales, counselling or other similar situations and we are thinking in different 'modes', isn't it going to be difficult to establish a meaningful rapport?

What is likely to occur is that a conversation between a person thinking **visually** and a person thinking in **feelings** could turn out to be a frustrating experience for both parties. The visual thinker will probably be tapping a foot impatiently, while the 'feeling' thinker literally 'won't see' why the other has to go so quickly. A positive result is likely to depend on who adapts to the other's way of thinking first.

So what does all this tell the manager about the relationship between body language and thought processes? Well, one thing is for sure; if you want to establish a rapport with someone, being 'on the same wavelength' is a good start. In the past, this might simply have meant responding as best as possible to how you feel the other person will react. Now, with the advantage of knowing that we think in different modes we can perhaps fine-tune our response by using similar words as the person we are talking to.

Body talk
Visual thinkers are more likely to use 'visual expressions' such as 'I *see* what you mean', 'Can we get that in *focus*', 'It seems *hazy* to me', whereas **auditory thinkers** would say such things as 'That *sounds* odd to me', 'I *hear* what you say' and so forth.

Kinesthetic thinkers, on the other hand, would say such things as 'It doesn't *feel* right to me', 'My *gut* reaction is to say no', or ' I can't *grasp* that idea'. By reflecting back the same words the sensitive manager can maintain rapport in such areas as selling, couselling, interviewing or appraising. Managers noted for their social skills will often be on the same wavelength as others because they consciously or subconsciously adopt the same speech patterns and words.

So, if you find yourself feeding back a few of the words that the other person is using because you feel that you are on common ground, it is probably due to your increasing awareness of them. You are becoming more **socially and emotionally intelligent**.

Actions speak louder than words
Posture and gesture

To a very large extent, we physically dance to the tune of our thoughts, conveying *meaning* and *feeling* through our actions. Gesticulations, head movements and body posture all add emphasis to what we are saying, investing our words with meaning, and adding to the impression we create.

Sometimes thoughts and feelings that we try to hide behind our words creep out in our posture and gestures. Not surprisingly, as listeners, we rely heavily on what someone's body language tells us before we make up our minds about them.

Many types of posture and a variety of gestures – such as the **raising of eyebrows** when we meet – are common to people of all cultures, while others, especially certain **hand gestures**, are culturally specific and you have to be a little careful how you use them in different countries.

UK & USA = O.K.

JAPAN = MONEY

BRAZIL = INSULT

FRANCE = ZERO

For example, in the USA, when the thumb and forefinger make a circle this means 'OK', while in Brazil it represents an insult similar to the British 'V' sign and the American raised middle finger. In Japan, however, it means 'money' and in France 'zero'.

In Europe, scratching your head can mean you are puzzled about something, whereas in Japan it is often an indication of anger.

> We not only make assumptions about people's moods and feelings from postures and gestures, but also tend to view those who exhibit a greater variety of body language in a more positive light. Studies have found that people who communicate non-verbally through **active movement** tend to be rated as **warm**, more **casual**, **agreeable** and **energetic**, while those who **remain still** are seen as **logical**, **cold** and **analytic**.

Posture

Anger, excitement, shyness, rejection

You can often tell a person's **attitude** from their body language. **Anger** tends to be conveyed by leaning forward, sometimes with fists clenched and a 'tight' facial expression. Excitement is often exhibited in an open body position, arms raised up, palms open, with mouth and eyes wide open. Shyness is usually conveyed by looking down, making little eye contact and leaning to one side, while rejection tends to be exhibited by turning the face and body away.

Intimidation

How a person **stands** can indicate not only how they feel, but also how they 'view' a situation – in other words, their **attitude towards** someone or something. A very upright (uptight?) stance can appear threatening, particularly when your territory (such as your office) is invaded by someone marching in and standing in close proximity to you.

Senior managers who act in this way towards their subordinates are, not surprisingly, seen as **intimidating**. So to maintain rapport with others it is advisable, particularly if you are tall, to reduce your height. Lean on something, stoop slightly.

People of high status often stand arms akimbo – hands on hips with elbows turned out. This is a posture of **superiority** and exemplifies **dominance**. Sitting with legs in

| Depressed | Rejecting | Excited |
| Defensive | Thoughtful | Confident |

Posture of superiority

the four-cross position (with the ankle of one leg resting on the knee of the other) with elbows outstretched and hands clasped behind the neck, head or back similarly suggest superiority. It is not uncommon to see two equal-status male managers in discussion subconsciously adopting similar postures in order to maintain their respective positions of authority.

Defensiveness
When you see someone sitting in a meeting with their arms crossed, what do you make of it? True, this often happens when chairs have no arm rests but it could mean that the person concerned is being **defensive**. Any hunching of the back or clenching of the fists – even if the individual is unaware that this is happening – can be interpreted as **aggressive-defensive**, or even **hostile**.

Interest – indifference

Posture not only reflects feelings, but also **intentions**.

People subconsciously indicate **positive interest** in others by propping their heads up on a hand with the index finger pointing up over the cheek. **Critical appraisal** is similarly indicated by an attentive gaze with the chin resting on a thumb and the fingers touching or covering the mouth.

Seated readiness posture

These are quite commonly observed in meetings among buyers or senior executives when they are evaluating other peoples' comments.

Leaning forwards in your chair suggests that you are **reacting positively** to what you are hearing and that you may be about to act upon a particular suggestion. On the other hand, leaning backwards tends to indicate **indifference**, or a lack of interest.

Inappropriate posture
Inappropriate body language can be insulting or annoying. Some people deliberately use it for this purpose. Coming over as too forceful or too relaxed can be offensive. For example, sitting slumped in a chair with your head down when someone is talking to you displays indifference towards the speaker. Similarly, sitting with one leg over the arm of a chair suggests casual indifference.

As a rule of thumb we would advise against the use of over-casual body language, particularly in situations where you are dealing with valued clients or subordinates.

Cultural differences can sometimes lead to erroneous conclusions about posture. American men, for example, often sit with their legs in a four-cross pattern. European men will often just cross one leg over the other, which is perceived in the USA as an effeminate posture!

Male body language in the company of women during meetings sometimes produces the unexpected. One study found that when a woman was present in a standing group, those men who were attracted to her pointed their feet in her direction – even when they were talking to their male colleagues.

Male pair and female pair exhibiting posture congruence

Copycat behaviour

We have already referred to posture congruence in which people imitate or mirror each other's posture, often without realising. **Interactional synchronising** occurs when people simultaneously move at the same time in the same way, such as picking up coffee cups or starting to speak at exactly the same moment – and this often occurs when people are getting on well together. It is almost as if people are 'echoing' one another; in fact, we are responding subliminally to our partners' subtle cues.

Opening up

It takes time for people to feel comfortable with a superior and, as many body language experts will testify, if you can get an individual to open up physically, the chances are that he or she will open up emotionally as well. Crossed arms, legs or ankles, self-hugging, chin down and a slumped appearance are all tell-tale signs that something is wrong.

Writing on the subject of bullying at work, the relationship specialist, Julie Hay, points out that: 'When you are bullied you may feel depressed and this makes you slump down and lean forward. If you try standing up straight instead, you can't feel depressed properly!' Conversely, she adds that when we feel angry we tense up, clench our fists and tighten the jaw, so that being persuaded to 'loosen up' can have the opposite effect of what is intended – 'you can't feel angry properly'.

What this means is that you need to find a way to break the ice gently. One way to do this is to offer tea or coffee. Though this may sound simplistic, it is nevertheless the case that people find it difficult to raise a cup to their mouths with their legs crossed, and almost totally impossible with their arms crossed. Thus, by such a simple procedure, you enable your 'closed' individual to literally 'open up'.

Gesture

If body posture **subconsciously** reflects feelings, mood and thought, gestures **consciously** convey emotion and meaning. This doesn't mean you know exactly what you are doing all of the time, rather it means that there is a greater degree of *conscious awareness* about your actions than in the case of body posture.

We generally gesture with our hands, arms, head and shoulders and do so to add emphasis to what we are saying.

Active interest, listening and concern
A common gesture of television interviewers and their guests is the head cock where the head is tilted to one side. This indicates **active listening**, interest and concern.

Nodding the head slowly while listening indicates 'I hear you and understand', whereas more rapid nods mean 'I hear you and agree with you.'

A word of warning to interviewers – the head nod that one generally regards as meaning 'yes', often means 'no' in Bulgaria, parts of Greece, Yugoslavia, Turkey, Iran and Bengal!

Confidence, aloofness, submission, aggression
Generally speaking, when the head is held up and the face points in an upward direction this indicates **confidence** and, in some cases, **aloofness**, or even a **patronising** attitude toward others. Lowering the head and avoiding eye contact is more suggestive of submissive behaviour. When someone thrusts their head and chin forward they may be signalling **alarm** or **aggressiveness**, particularly if the eyes are wide open at the same time.

Don't care, waste of time
A common shoulder gesture is the shrug where both are raised and often accompanied by the palms up hand gesture. These usually indicate that the person concerned **doesn't care**, **doesn't know**, or thinks whatever is happening is **a waste of time.**

Disagreement
Certain gestures that we use can appear at variance with what we are saying. Take the case where a listener tells the speaker that they are in agreement yet the former's head appears to move slightly from side to side rather than up or down thus signalling *dis*agreement. In such cases it may be that the listener simply cannot be bothered to argue – in other words, his or her real feelings are indicated by the head shake.

While some individuals will show disagreement by shaking their heads, others do so less obviously by 'picking lint' – picking imaginary pieces of fluff off their clothes. Whether consciously intended or not, this conveys the message '**I disagree with you, but I can't be bothered to argue about it.**'

Hand gestures

The handshake – strength or weakness?
Between countries and cultures similar gestures have different meanings and can easily give rise to misunderstandings. For example, one of the most commonly used gestures in organisational life is the handshake.

Whereas in the USA and western Europe a **firm handshake** is associated with positiveness, conviction, strength, openness and honesty, in the Indian sub-continent a **limp handshake** is the norm, representing a different perception of what is positive.

Hand-cupping – domination and control
Hand gestures can be used to express negative as well as positive feelings, such as annoyance, aggression and insult. People who choose to shake hands by placing one hand over – rather than to the side of – the other person's hand are wanting to assert their dominance.

Fist and finger insults
Fist waving, the 'V' sign and the single finger pointing upwards are all insults. In fact, **pointing** – known as **battoning** – is generally regarded as rude or aggressive and should be avoided wherever possible in the context of business interaction. It is more socially acceptable to direct

an upraised palm than to point towards someone when in a meeting.

Though in much of Europe tapping the forefinger on the side of the head is widely recognised as signifying 'you're crazy', the Dutch tap the centre of the forehead, while the French 'screw' the finger into the side of the head.

The hand shrug – mock honesty
In conversation a palms-up gesture tends to indicate **uncertainty,** though with a degree of **honesty.** But it can also be used to deceive. The **hand-shrug**, as it is known, is one of those **mock honesty** gestures which appear to enlist our sympathy by giving the impression that the other person has our best interests at heart despite being unsure of the outcome.

Patting, tapping, thumping, fiddling
When someone places their hands palms-down in a 'patting' fashion, along with raised eyebrows, they are

Mock honesty

'Trust me – I'm in marketing'

probably indicating **satisfaction** with, or **certainty** about the facts placed before them. If this 'patting' continues it most likely means 'I have heard what you have to say so please calm down.' Tapping one's fingers on a desk is a clear sign of impatience while banging or thumping clearly indicates **annoyance** and **aggression**. Fiddling with pencils during meetings suggests **boredom** or **irritation**.

Steepling – confidence, certainty
A common gesture often seen in organisational life is steepling, where both hands are close together with finger tips touching, but with palms a short distance apart – quite literally in the shape of a church steeple.

Steepling

Often unconsciously performed, this action has been interpreted as indicating a sense of **confidence**, or as suggesting that the individual concerned has come to a **decision**. Clearly this has significance in the sales situation.

Palm rocking – 'maybe'
Another hand gesture often noticed among younger

managers is palm rocking with fingers spread out. Amusingly termed the 'so-so' it involves the palm being face down and rocked from side to side. This is taken to mean something similar to the verbal '-ish', meaning 'maybe', 'possibly', 'ok-ish'.

Thumbs up
You would think that the ubiquitous 'thumbs up' gesture would be commonly understood as meaning '**O.K.**', 'everything's fine' and so forth, but it isn't. In Australia, if made with a jerk, it means '**up yours!**', and in Nigeria it is also regarded as rude. In Germany, when you order drinks, it means '**one please**'.

Deception gestures

Rubbing, scratching, touching
There are gestures of which we are hardly aware, such as touching our noses when we **are not telling the truth**, or when we believe someone is trying to deceive us.

Scratching one's neck with the index finger about five times below the ear, while the neck is turned slightly to one side, indicates **doubt and uncertainty**. This gesture is common among car mechanics who also tend to suck in air between the teeth when asked how long it will take and how much it will cost to repair your car!

Sometimes when people are **not telling the truth** they rub their eye while looking down as if they are distracted by a piece of grit, when in fact this gesture is designed to distract the attention of the listener.

When you see someone tap the side of their nose with their

forefinger this can indicate a desire for **confidentiality** or **secrecy**, although the gesture differs in meaning between cultures.

In Britain and Sardinia, the nose tap conveys **complicity, confidentiality**, or **secrecy**, while in Italy it means be alert. In Britain, Holland and Austria, if the tap is to the front of the nose it means **mind your own business.**

In some situations, placing a hand over the nose suggests both fear and disbelief – as if one does not wish to comprehend or accept what is going on.

So you see, the body language of posture and gesture really can be quite revealing. One thing's for sure, you'll never take it for granted again.

Keep it a secret

Power and influence

The road to success

Success has as much to do with being seen to do your job well as actually doing it well. It's a simple (although perhaps not always welcome) fact of life that conveying the right impression can make up for deficiencies in knowledge and skills. Many talented people fail to gain promotion because they make the mistake of thinking that success is judged on the basis of **what** they do well, rather than the **impression** they create in doing it.

As we have already seen on Monday, understanding body language can make managers more effective. **Effective leaders** not only spend time on the task in hand, but also on the needs of the individuals who make up the team. Sensitivity to such needs increases effectiveness and influence – advantages achieved as a result of enhanced interpersonal skills.

By not understanding the subtleties of body language you are at a disadvantage in the communication process. A lack of awareness of the non-verbal signals that people give automatically limits your **insight** into their behaviour and intentions.

The body language of power

Many of the words we use to describe interaction with authority figures reflect characteristics of the body language of power. For example, an influential member of staff may be said to be 'close to the boss', when the boss allows that person to occupy his or her **physical space**. When we say 'she has the boss's ear' (or eye for that matter), we mean she is close enough to say things in private. 'He's the boss's right-hand man' not only signifies **personal influence**, but **close liaison** with the person in authority.

Some individuals try to influence their superiors by adopting a **subservient** approach. This can result in derogatory comments about 'crawling', or being 'a creep' – characteristics of behaviour which Dickens epitomised in the character of the obsequious Uriah Heep from *David Copperfield*. The clear indication is that people who lower themselves physically diminish the respect accorded to them. **Pushy** people, on the other hand, are often those who 'try to get round the boss', thereby **gaining access** to authority at the expense of others.

When we describe someone as 'straight', we mean open and honest, while '**bent**' signifies the opposite. Similarly, someone who is 'upright' is to be **trusted**, and the person who 'walks tall' feels confident and proud. Individuals who see others as inferior 'look down on' or 'down their noses at' them. Lifting the head slightly whilst doing this is an expression of contempt. All these terms refer to the postures associated with power or the lack of it.

'Keeping someone at arm's length' or 'not crowding their space' literally means not getting **too close** to them'. We often take these words and phrases for granted without realising that they are descriptions of body language cues that we witness all the time.

Powerbroking

People get where they are because they adopt different

strategies for increasing their authority over others. Among these are **five sources of power**, as described by French and Raven.

- *position* – who they are
- *coercive* – how tough they are
- *reward* – how supportive they are
- *expertise* – how informed they are
- *charisma* – how unique they are

Position power

John Title

'My power in this organisation comes from people knowing who I am. I'm a Senior Supervisor and this means that staff should respect my authority. We should look up to our superiors, after all that's what **'super'** = **'above'** + **'visor'** = **'look'** means. Others look up to me. I have access to the boss because of my position in the company.

Powerbrokers who rely upon **who they are** in the organisation are not difficult to spot. They adopt the postures, gestures and unspoken cues associated with hierarchical authority. The most casual of observers will generally be able to pick out the 'boss' in a group by the respective body language of superior and subordinate. Typically the boss will adopt a 'posture of superiority' or will look down their nose at others.

The significant thing about position power is that it is the minimum form of authority that a manager has. People still tend to obey managers out of respect for the title – even if the individual fails in all other aspects of the job.

Power and status symbols – like one's own office, car, uniform, carpet or where you sit in the restaurant – can be used to advantage. Common power gestures include hands on hips, arms akimbo, holding the lapel with thumbs up, or hands in pockets with thumbs out, head up looking down the nose and so on.

A manager we came across used to make people wait outside his door for longer than might be expected after they had knocked, and then shout 'come in!' in an irritated tone. This had the effect of making the employee feel uncomfortable about entering the manager's **territory**. The manager would continue writing, thus giving the impression that he was not to be disturbed. After a further period he would look up slowly whilst replacing his pen-top and, with a degree of impatience, tell the unfortunate individual to go back and close the door. Through his body language and tone of voice he reminded his **subordinate** of their **relative positions.**

In recent years, cyclical changes in general economic conditions have brought about a fundamental reappraisal of organisational structures and patterns of employment, with the result that attitudes to hierarchical authority have altered. **Horizontal** (expertise) rather than **vertical** (position) lines of authority make for greater cooperation and encourage up-skilling.

The acceptance of a more egalitarian approach to employment and management has been shown to increase personal commitment to employers and to boost production. By reducing status barriers, communication is increased and flexibility in working practices is encouraged.

At the MARS company in Slough, England, for example, employees wear the same uniform – to emphasise greater equality and hence less of a distinction between superiors and subordinates. Some large organisations in the UK, such as the Eastern Group and Eli Lilly, have done away with the term 'manager' altogether, preferring instead designations such as coach, team member and team leader that emphasise team spirit. Managers these days are expected to **facilitate** not merely **administrate**. In the future, the term 'manager' may well disappear, as the terms foreman, charge-hand and supervisor are slowly disappearing. The decay of these terms means the **decay of position power** and the **rise of reward power and expert power.**

Coercive power

Phil Hardman

'You have to be tough and decisive to manage. If managers fail to take on, or to discipline idle employees they won't be respected by the rest of the workforce.

Threats enhance respect for a manager. How many times have you heard someone say 'He's fair, but I wouldn't get *on the wrong side* of him if I were you'.

The strong manager doesn't 'um and err' about things, or ask if everything's OK with you. Just hold your gaze; **stand straight and don't move around** – because it suggests you are wavering.'

The body language of coercion is not difficult to recognise – its most common expression being **aggression**, which is characterised by overt postures and gestures that are designed to threaten, such as:

- the upright stance, standing with hands on hips, or sitting in a dominant position
- an expressionless or angry gaze
- the invasion of another's space
- shouting
- finger-pointing (battoning)
- staring at a subordinate
- 'strutting' (down corridors) in a way that conveys the impression that no one will get in your way
- turning away when someone else is talking
  - peppering conversation with snorts of derision, annoyance or disgust
  - frowning, or jutting the chin out
  - clenching the fist.

However, coercive power can also be **self-defeating**. **Threats** (negative appraisal, demotion) and **non-verbal intimidation** (invasion of personal space, the upright stance, staring) can mean that the manager will not enjoy a loyal and motivated workforce and will have to bear the extra cost of high staff turnover.

To resort to coercive methods when the situation genuinely requires it – firing someone for gross misconduct – may be acceptable, although you need to be aware of your motives. Be sure that coercion is not being used to boost your own ego. In the long run, the **latent threat** of coercive action tends to prove more effective.

Finger pointing or battoning

Reward power

Jill Merit

'Staff in my company obey their superiors because they know that they will ultimately be **rewarded** in some way. The culture promotes this. Perhaps we're different, but we know how to keep our employees happy. It's not bribery, it's **sympathetic management**.

We are not in a position to increase salaries at the drop of a hat, but we can reward people with more interesting work, a glowing appraisal, more responsibility, giving them a sense of achievement, and empowering them.

Unlike monetary rewards, psychological encouragement is conveyed non-verbally through tone of voice and gestures and needs to be sincere if it is to have the desired effect of motivating and boosting morale. There are many ways in which managers can reward employees in this way. For example:

- the longer than average handshake or the handclasp to emphasise a job well done
- a light touch or pat on the back to express praise or congratulation – touching someone on the shoulder as they leave is a subtle way of rewarding good rapport
- the smile and a slightly longer gaze to denote thanks
- a slight nod of the head to suggest agreement or recognition.

We often use **body language expressions** with reference to rewarding people without necessarily realising the connection between the emotion and the physical action – 'I was touched'; 'I had to hand it to her'; 'it was only a small gesture'; 'he deserves a pat on the back for that'.

Expert power

Dr Graham Sure

'Being recognised as **experts** in our field increases our **influence** and **control**. How else do you think we get our research funding? This is where the advantages of body language come in. If I appear hesitant, look puzzled, fail to make adequate eye contact, speak without self-assurance, come across as non-assertive and lacking in confidence, this makes people question my competence, because I **appear** unsure.

Non-expert	Expert
I **hope** that you will enjoy this presentation.	I know that you will appreciate what I have to say.
I **think** that is most **probably** the answer	Under these circumstances **this** is what **we should do**.

The emphasis placed on these words is all important.'

Assertive body language conveys **confidence** and suggests **expertise**. The way you stand, or the manner in which you pay attention to others gives an impression of certainty, self-assurance and a sense that you 'feel good about yourself'. Simple things like fixing your gaze on the other person and 'steepling' – where the finger tips are touching but the palms are apart – show that you are interested in what you are being told. This kind of relaxed body language exudes confidence. Turning the hands palms-down and appearing to press downwards while talking to others also has the effect of making others listen and look up to you.

Research in **Neuro-linguistic Programming** has shown that we condition ourselves to succeed or fail by our thought processes. By '**self-conditioning**' – maintaining an internal dialogue that reinforces personal successes – we can make ourselves **feel more confident**, thereby making us more influential. Confident words should be used with confident posture and gesture:

- use positive-sounding words and emphasise your certainty at all times
- when talking, hold the palms down to express certainty
- when sitting, use the 'steeple' position of the hands (palms apart, fingertips touching) to show you are 'in touch' with what is going on
- stand upright, maintain an 'open' stance and smile
- walk with an upright posture as if you know the place and where you are going
- keep your head up, but don't look down your nose
- precondition yourself to succeed. Above all, have faith in yourself and your abilities.

Charisma

A Fan

'When he walked into the room I was mesmerised. I couldn't take my eyes off him. I don't know what it was. He had a sort of aura, a self-assurance without arrogance – a **presence**.

He didn't even have to speak. There were people buzzing around him like flies and yet he seemed totally unconcerned. I was the one feeling nervous.

How lucky to be like that. Some people just have that indefinable quality, don't they? That *je ne sais quoi*.'

Social psychologists have long tried to establish the link between **leadership** and **charisma** and have found that charisma itself resides in the minds of the followers not in the traits of the leader.

This means that it is **our perceptions** of a colleague's or competitor's abilities that invest that individual with charismatic power rather than the abilities themselves. So, we should be seeking evidence of 'charismatic body language' in the audience – among the believers.

When a charismatic person enters a room others move away to give him or her **space**. Sometimes it is simply the hush that descends on the gathering that tells you someone is highly regarded. Charismatic people often **seem tall** to the observer because individuals tend to bow slightly – literally lowering their height in front of their 'leader'. Charismatic people are also said to radiate power, energy, love and so forth, and yet this radiation comes from the audience in response to the admired person.

'Charismatic authority', therefore, is a 'social' property – **invested** in the highly regarded or venerated individual **by others**, and **maintained by that individual** through **constant reinforcement** of those characteristics most admired.

Sometimes we refer to these special people as being 'head and shoulders above the rest'. These are the ones who are 'up front', 'firm', 'rock steady', even 'having us in the palms of their hands'. We respect them for their leadership, aware that there is something about their **presence** that denotes authority.

More on assertiveness

We now wish to explain assertiveness and its value in terms of body language.

There are four 'styles' of behaviour that all of us characterise from time to time: **aggressive, submissive, assertive** and **manipulative**. Some people are disproportionately more aggressive or submissive than others and, as a result, tend to be thought of in these terms.

Assertiveness basically means 'declaring your position in a firm, open and reasonable manner'. The professional manager who is 'firm, but fair' generally feels more confident about handling difficult situations, improves business outcomes, gets the best out of other people and actually reduces conflict with and between them. Often this means that he or she is able to manage without words, to make others aware of his or her views and feelings via the subtle nuances of body language.

There is little doubt that **managerial effectiveness** can be enhanced by a greater understanding of body language. Successful managers are those who feel comfortable about being assertive and display their expertise and leadership qualities through **self-assured** and **confident behaviour**.

The body language of power

- **Aggressive**

Description	Body language
Angry, sarcastic, being a bad listener, putting people down, blaming others, shouting, speaking in a raised voice, critical etc.	Clenched fists, confrontational pose, tense body posture, hands on hips, head tilted, finger-pointing, prolonged eye contact narrowing eyes, looking down on others.

• Manipulative

Description

Patronising, crafty, calculating, insincere, two-faced, a 'user', lacking trust, over-friendly, making ends justify means, contrived etc.

Body language

Exaggerated gestures (eg open palms to indicate 'deliberate' sincerity) overly laid-back, posture, 'patronising' touching, exaggerated eye contact, 'sugary' voice tone, patting.

• Submissive

Description

Apologetic, self-deprecating, resentful, low self-esteem, retreating, overly ready to please.

Body language

Fidgety, covering mouth and eyes, imitative, slumped posture, nervous disposition, fiddling, poor eye contact, quiet, faltering voice, 'pleading' smile, tendency to obsequiousness.

• Assertive

Description

Sincere, open, honest, respectful, sympathetic, firm but fair, offering constructive criticism, good listener, offering praise where it is due, treating people as equals.

Body language

Upright relaxed posture, face-to-face eye contact, calm and open gestures, relaxed facial expression, maintaining reasonable distance from subject (not too close for comfort), resonant speech, unambiguous hand signals.

Performance art

Presentation skills

'Brilliance without the capability to communicate it is worth little in any enterprise,' wrote Thomas Leech in 1982.

Every presentation you make is essentially a **performance**, in which the hearts and minds of the audience are there to be won over. As we noted earlier, as much as 90% of what we communicate is transmitted non-verbally, which means that a large part of our performance relies upon **presence**, as distinct from words, technical support or gimmickry. No matter how many visual aids you have at your disposal, nothing is ultimately as visually persuasive as **yourself.**

It is perhaps no accident that highly successful presenters are described as having their audiences 'in the palm of their hands', when you consider that the 'up-turned palm' has traditionally been associated with gestures of honesty, openness and sincerity.

Before beginning a presentation make sure you know what you are trying to do. For example, do you aim to inform, instruct, persuade, entertain, justify, or sell? The objective must be clear to you but not necessarily clear to the audience.

Salespeople know that by overstating their intention to sell, they increase the resistance on the part of their clients to buy. But by subtle use of body language and tone of voice you can convince an audience that you are simply there to inform.

The ten rules of engagement

1   Maintain eye contact with the audience.
Members of your audience need to believe that you are
talking to each of them as individuals. They need to feel
that your 'random glance' during a sweep of the room is at
them in particular and that you are only looking at
everyone else out of politeness.

Remember presenters who maintain regular eye contact with
the audience are more likely to be perceived as being
persuasive, sincere, credible, honest, experienced and friendly.

2   Be aware of hand gestures and tone of voice
If eye contact is important in gaining the attention of your
audience, how you **act** and **sound** is just as important in
maintaining it. Your hands should conduct your
presentation as if it were the slow movement of a
symphony, fingers and palms modulating with your words.

When presenting facts, it helps to hold the hands out and
the palms down as this indicates **assurance** and **certainty**.

The facts are as follows

Conversely, if you hold your palms upwards when delivering facts you may be perceived as **uncertain** and your message as confusing.

Speak slowly, adding **emphasis** where appropriate by varying the **tone** and **resonance** of your voice. Speaking more quickly to make a particular point is fine providing that your audience can hear and understand you. Very often presenters speed up when they start to feel confident about the presentation and 'lose' sections of the audience as a result.

3 Repeat key phrases to reinforce your message
One way of adding **emphasis** in a presentation is to repeat key phrases using an **assertive tone** of voice. The *actual* words themselves need not always be repeated providing that the *meaning* remains the same. In selling, for example, one might say, 'There are **four** main selling points to this product. The **four points** are ... Let us look in detail at **one** and then go through the other **three points**.

4 Use visual aids to structure your presentation
Maintaining eye contact with the audience while making use of prompting techniques and facilities is not always easy. One method is to use cards, which are held in the palm of the hand and require you to take your eyes off the audience only momentarily. These cards should contain only **key words** – reminders of what you wish to say – and nothing else.

Another, and perhaps better, way is to use words on the screen or flip chart as **key word prompts** and as a means of structuring your presentation. Structuring can also be done by means of a flip-chart agenda, which enables you to 'signpost' issues and ideas that indicate your intention to move from one area to the next. Typical expressions that you would use in such situations might be 'moving on now to item three', or 'I would now like to examine the outcome'.

Whatever you do, **do not allow a visual aid to distract you from those you are addressing**. The moment you start to pay less attention to the audience, the audience starts to pay less attention to you.

The audience will pay less attention to you if you turn your back

5   Be animated but stay calm and look professional.

There are a number of common distractions that reduce audience attention. For example, **do not**:

- **march** from one side of the stage to the other
- **fiddle** with pointers, pens and other sundry items
- **seek confirmation** with phrases like 'Is that O.K?', 'Do you see?' or 'You know what I mean?'

- stand with your **hands in your pockets**; the posture gives the impression that you are over-confident; but more importantly if your hands are in your pockets you cannot use them to gesture and emphasise your words.

6   Hold audience attention by sounding enthusiastic

It is generally accepted that for all presentations there is an **attention curve**. Audience attention will be high at the beginning, low in the middle and higher at the end. If your presentation is long – more than thirty minutes – you should try to hold their attention by sounding more enthusiastic as you go along. **Enthusiasm** is powerfully expressed through body language and can be **infectious**.

7   Retain attention by having a natural break
Another way of retaining attention is to have a natural break in the middle of your presentation, for example by passing round items, samples and literature. But if you are going to do this, keep the materials hidden from view at the start otherwise they will distract attention away from you.

8   Take note of negative body language
The more skilled that you become in recognising the meanings implicit in gesture and posture, the more control you will have over your audience. Certain gestures and postures tell you a lot about people's attitude towards you and their **receptiveness** to what you are saying:

- Leaning the chin on a hand with the index finger on the cheek indicates **critical appraisal** or critical evaluation.

- The steepling gesture indicates that someone has **made up their minds** either for or against you.
- Sitting with arms and ankles crossed indicates that someone may feel **defensive.**
- Picking lint from clothes indicates that someone disagrees but does not want to argue with you.

If you are aware of these things happening, try to draw the people concerned into the dialogue. One method of doing this is to invite comments from the audience by directing your line of sight to the individual who seems out of favour with what you are saying. For example: 'I'm sure I haven't convinced all of you, so perhaps, you Sir/Madam ... what sort of concerns do you feel people might have about this?' By keeping your question impersonal you are more likely to get them to drop their defences and air their views.

Critical appraisal

Picking lint: silent disagreement

9   Avoid being distracted by members of the audience
Because body language is a two-way process, presenters, whether they are aware of it or not, **respond to cues and signals** given by members of the audience. There are three common pitfalls associated with this:

- *the 'friendly' individual* who is clearly paying attention and who nods and occasionally smiles in response to the presenter's points. The presenter may unwittingly direct his or her attention to that individual, thus breaking the visual link with the rest of the audience.
- the one-to-one conversation where the presenter gets caught up in a question-and-answer situation with a single member of the audience. All too often this makes other members of the audience feel excluded.

10   Attempt to encourage convergence of opinions
In any audience there are bound to be differences of

opinion and the astute presenter can often identify sets or subgroups of people who appear to share similar opinions. This is particularly important in negotiations or meetings in which the goal is to achieve a consensus.

As we have already observed, when people establish a rapport they often mirror each other's gestures and postures (posture congruence). For example, you might be in a meeting in which three people from Personnel and Accounts appear to be sharing the same body posture. The group of engineers over the other side of the table, however, are sitting, straight-backed, with arms folded. What do you make of this? Do you conclude that the engineers are being defensive and that their body language indicates that a lot of work still needs to be done before they are won over? If so, what is your strategy for dealing with the situation?

What you need to do is to **encourage participation**.

- Mention their names or describe their expertise. Even if you think that you have to sound ingratiating or flattering about people's skills and contributions, it is worth remembering that most people like to be respected and given credence for their views.
- Produce more support for your ideas. This can be done by using the technique previously described as upward appeal. In this case, you would introduce the following kinds of statements: 'The Managing Director and I had a long discussion about this very point and he agrees with me . . .',

It is worth remembering that every presentation is

Personnel   Accounts

essentially a performance and **how you perform** is central
to the success or failure of what you are trying to
communicate.

Selling yourself

There is a well-known, though unwritten, rule in Sales that to be effective you need to sell yourself before you can successfully sell your product. **Selling is communication**; since most of the communication process is non-verbal, the type of body language you adopt is likely to make all the difference between success and failure.

The interaction that takes place between buyer and seller has often been the subject of caricature. This is because buyers have money and power while sellers need to sell to justify their role. While selling is a service the sales person will fail to achieve success if perceived as servile. Dickens' Uriah Heep portrayed himself as 'the 'umblest person going', but his servility was essentially manipulative, and buyers don't like being manipulated.

Subservience personified

The ground rules

The five **examples of power** that we discussed on Tuesday
– **position, coercion, reward, expertise** and **charisma** –
equally apply to you in the sales situation, though with a
difference of emphasis.

1   Remember who you are
(position power)

Sellers generally have less power than buyers for the simple
reason that buyers can say 'yes', 'no', or even, 'convince
me'. Over the years, business practice has come to
recognise the status differentials between buyers and sellers
with the result that more 'significant' titles have been
invented to take account of the relative lack of **position
power** of sales personnel. Gone are the days when you
would wield the small white card saying Sales
Representative. Today, you are more likely to carry the title
Regional Sales Director, X & Y Consultant, or Account
Director.

There is always a danger that if you don't recognise the
relative lack of power in your position as a seller, you will
offend, put off, or irritate the client. Taking account of this
displays your recognition of the other party's need to be
respected for showing interest in you and your product. So
you don't keep the buyer waiting and you don't allow your
body language to convey messages of urgency, aggression,
arrogance or insincerity.

This means that you should maintain a **respectable
distance** from the client (between two and four feet), **alter
your standing posture** so as not to give the impression of

towering over your client. Door-to-door sales personnel are actually told to step back when someone opens the door. This indicates that they are **non-threatening** and have no intention of invading the client's space.

Having established your position in the transaction, how you speak to the client is all-important. Much of what you **convey** is via **tone and speed of voice,** indicating sincerity, trust and reliability.

2 *Make the client feel comfortable*
(reward power)

Making the client feel comfortable is an essential part of establishing a good rapport. Some sales personnel find that **making notes** during the course of a meeting helps to reinforce the status of the buyer by making him or her **feel** more important. Others bring gifts and free samples with them – think of all the pens and pads that medical reps leave behind in GP clinics.

> If you give something to another person, however small, there is an obligation on their part to want to agree with you or buy your product. We knew a manager once who would always offer a colleague a mint before he asked them a favour, once they took the mint they found it difficult to say no.

It goes without saying that the interaction between buyer and seller should be **rewarding** to the buyer (that is if you want to see him or her again). Hence the mannerisms adopted by the seller should always be polite and **respectful**, though not overtly ingratiating.

Selling is a sophisticated business and without **self-assurance** and a **convincing manner** no amount of information, gifts or promises will work for you. A relaxed manner and a sense of humour are often all that are needed to win the day.

A relaxed manner will win the day

If the seller makes the buyer feel like **a valued customer** it is a subtle way of rewarding his or her continuing interest. Also, the product itself is a type of reward in that, with the right deal, it fulfils the buyer's requirements.

3   Persuasion, not coercion
(coercive power)

If rewarding the buyer is part of the psychology of successful selling then it stands to reason that coercion is not. You seek to **persuade**, not **bully** or **manipulate**. The buyer, on the other hand, might use coercive power to try to manipulate you and this is when you need all your faculties about you.

The coercive buyer can get away with being aggressive

towards you, being rude when it suits them and winding you up just to see how far you can be pushed. Often such people will use postures and gestures which reinforce their coercive power. This is because clients have **purchasing power** and it is your job to serve them. You may be seething under the surface, but if you keep your cool, you will come out the winner.

By taking note of the buyer's body language, you will soon learn how to interpret it. For example:

- *Superiority* can be deduced from a posture in which the hands are clasped round the back of the head with the elbows pointing out sideways.
- *Critical evaluation* tends to be indicated by the chin leaning on an upward-pointing index finger.
- *Impatience* is shown by fingers drumming on a hard surface, combined with sideways glances and snorts of disagreement.
- *Disagreement* or even disbelief is shown by shaking the head slightly from side to side.
- *Understanding* is shown by a slow nodding of the head while nodding more quickly indicates agreement.
- *Confidence* and having made up one's mind is indicated by steepling.

Successful salespeople want long-term relationships with clients. Some enjoy getting new business **(hunters)** while others like to revisit clients regularly **(gatherers)**.

4   *Be cautious about being the expert*
(expert power)

Selling undoubtedly relies upon expertise, although care

needs to be taken before playing the expert. The seller may know considerably more about the product than the buyer but it is often better to play this down and to let the buyer feel confident and knowledgeable about the subject.

Sometimes the buyer will convey a sense of 'giving way to' the seller's expertise, but this may be as much to 'test out' the substance of the seller's knowledge and experience as to learn about the product.

Noting the **tone of voice** can make all the difference here. If, for example, the buyer says 'I see, tell me more', do you take this to mean

(a) *I am interested, carry on.*

(b) *I'll humour him/her for the moment, but I'm not convinced.*

(c) *I do not believe you for one moment.*

The **real meaning** behind the buyer's questions are in the **tone of voice** not the words.

Your response to ambiguity of this kind needs to be positive and should seek to **affirm** what you have already been saying. Open body language is all-important here. You want to come across as **confident** and **assertive**, so:

• maintain eye contact
• smile (but don't grimace)
• keep an upright, open body stance
• remember that 'palms down' expresses certainty.

Whatever you do, have faith in yourself. There is nothing

worse than looking down as this suggests resignation or defeat. Equally, fidgeting can be seen as shiftiness and the client may lose trust in you.

If the buyer does not have the expertise and knowledge about the product or service and clearly indicates that you are the expert, then here is your chance to adopt the **consultant style** of selling where you solve their problems and difficulties as part of the sales process. The consultative style is shown through **assertive gestures** and **postures** and more **confidence in the tone of voice**.

5   *Be sincere, look the part*
(charismatic power)

Successful salespeople tend to be outgoing and often extrovert individuals. Some are genuinely charismatic and exude enthusiasm and charm and have little difficulty in securing the interest of their clients. Others work hard on their presentation skills to make up for any lack of spontaneity. In both cases, what makes them successful is their **sincerity**, and they achieve this by **matching their body language with their words**.

Remember charisma is **in the mind of the beholder** or, in this case, the buyer. What's more, charisma on its own is not necessarily a touchstone to sales success, so do not *try* to be charismatic; just develop your expert and reward power and the charisma will develop itself.

Body language in telephone selling

If you watch colleagues talking on the telephone, some of them will feel as if they are in face-to-face contact with the person on the other end of the line. Body posture and gesture tend to be reflected in the tone of voice, so adopting the wrong posture, even on the telephone, can give the wrong impression to the listener.

The point is that most telephone communication is restricted to para-linguistic cues; what you think and how you feel are conveyed through **voice intonation**. And it is how you **sound** at the other end that determines the type of reaction. The word 'phoney' actually derives from the sensation (first described during the early days of the telephone) of mistrusting the disembodied voice.

Body posture certainly conveys information about the telephone caller. It has been observed that people tend to lower their height slightly when talking to a superior on the phone.

It goes without saying that the salesperson should sound confident, friendly and enthusiastic, but this can be quite difficult in the context of a 'cold call' where the individual you are calling doesn't know you. One way round this situation is to 'psych' yourself up by deliberately adopting a **positive frame of mind** and an **assertive body posture** before you start the call. Not only will this make you **sound more self-assured**, but it will also make you feel more **confident**. For example:

- *Try standing with your head up* as you speak rather than sitting slumped at a desk.
- *Smile* when you talk, it comes across in your voice.
- *Reflect the other person's speed and tone of voice*; most of us do this automatically as it is a way of making us feel similar to, or on the same 'wavelength' as the client. Needless to say, if the client is

aggressive, abrupt, or has a voice impediment this could be self-defeating.

- *Tune in to the client's way of thinking.* As we saw on Monday, people tend to 'think' in three main ways: sight, sound and feeling. By recognising the particular kind of language – images – being used, the salesperson can subtly alter his or her approach to the client, thus increasing the chances of getting on the same wavelength.

The client's territory

When you enter the client's territory you are almost certainly at a disadvantage and as such you will probably touch your cuffs or your watch with one hand as a mild **defence mechanism**. As a rule of thumb, it is advisable to arrive early and to avoid sitting down on the chairs and sofas provided in the reception area. This is because being seated lowers your position whereby shaking hands and making eye contact becomes more difficult. Also, sitting down can give the impression of lacking respect for the client's authority.

The buyer's office
Going onto a client's territory is one thing, but entering the inner sanctum of the office is another. Since business is about buying and selling, and since we know that the seller needs to respect the buyer's status in order to give the right impression, body language now counts for a great deal.

- Standing too upright or too close to the client comes across as too **pushy** or **aggressive** so lower your height slightly.
- Standing less than two feet from your client is **too intimate** and nine feet is **too impersonal**, the correct

A mild defence mechanism

distance is between **two and four feet**. (In Arab cultures closer proximity is acceptable, so be aware of cultural differences.)

- Be aware of posture congruence and interactional synchronising: adopt similar body postures and gestures but do not deliberately copy as it comes across as contrived. Probably the best method is to use **cross-over mirroring** whereby the seller imitates the buyer's hand gestures with head movements.
- Never adopt a more relaxed posture than the buyer; remember your position power.
- The desk is **intimate territory** so get permission before you place your documents on it and be careful when leaning over it.
- Use **active listening** gestures, such as the **head cock**, or **grunts** and **nods** of agreement.
- **Maintain eye contact** with the buyer to be seen as more honest, persuasive, informed and credible.
- Be aware of hand gestures. Remember that **palms up**

indicates honesty or uncertainty, while **palms down** conveys certainty and assuredness.

- If the buyer has adopted the '**steepling**' gesture it may mean they have come to a decision. It is important for the seller to mentally note what gestures and comments preceded 'steepling' as this indicates possible success or failure in the transaction.

Summary

To deliberately use body language as an aid to selling is to miss the point. You are **not acting**, you are **understanding and utilising** your own natural attributes to your best advantage.

The truth detectives

Uncovering deception

Those who investigate the honesty of others need to be able to spot the **tell-tale signs** of deception without making it obvious that they are doing so. To some extent this relies upon **common sense** and **intuition**, although **training** is needed to develop and improve the skills. Part of such training involves the recognition of **body language clues** – the non-verbal indicators of concealment, falsification and lying.

Paradoxically, people involved in deception usually try to **avoid lying** by initially attempting to conceal the truth. For example, they may:
- fail to answer the question asked
- pretend not to understand it
- remain silent
- feign emotion, such as anger
- pretend they are feeling ill.

If they can't get away with concealing what they are doing, they may then begin to falsify the situation by:
- inventing a scenario
- telling a tall story
- telling a lie.

To conceal or avoid telling **direct lies** people will often water down their statements. Richard Nixon's famous counter to the allegation that he authorised the Watergate break-in – 'The President would not do such a thing.' – is a classic example of this. By depersonalising the act – taking the 'I' out of the equation – he absolved himself of responsibility for it.

For those whose task it is to elicit the truth from individuals suspected of deception, the type of questions asked and the nature of the answers given is all important. People generally try to water down lies so they sound less blatant.

Stress – the body language of deception
The body language of deception has its own particular signature – stress. This is manifested in mannered behaviour that seems out of place, or uncharacteristic of the individual. As early as 1905 Sigmund Freud wrote: 'He that has eyes to see and ears to hear may convince himself that no mortal can keep a secret. If his lips are silent, he chatters with his fingertips. Betrayal oozes out of every pore.'

Stress can indicate deception through:

- making odd facial expressions
- feigning yawns
- rubbing hands together
- picking fingernails
- stretching
- avoiding avoid eye contact
- pausing for longer than usual, or going silent
- exhibiting glazed expressions
- repeatedly clearing the throat
- making speech errors
- alternating the pitch of the voice
- grinding teeth or biting lips
- nose touching.

In some cases, individuals under suspicion decrease their normal expressive hand and arm movements, using them instead to soothe the nose, mouth and brow. 'Picking lint' can also be seen as characteristic of guilty behaviour.

The anxiety associated with deceiving others can have the following effects:

- shortness of breath
- difficulty in swallowing
- dry mouth
- flushing or blanching of the face
- sweating and palpitations.

In extreme circumstances the liar's body may even appear frozen, with arms and legs tightly folded in a defensive posture.

Postscript on nose touching
It is well known that when people tell lies or even hear other people lying they tend to touch their nose. There seems to be two explanations for this gesture. Firstly, by touching the nose the hand covers the mouth where the lies are coming from – children often cover their mouths when telling lies. Secondly when people tell lies it causes stress, and stress causes the skin to get slightly hotter (basis of the lie detector machine). When the skin gets hotter the nose, which is a sensitive organ, may itch or expand slightly so the individual touches the itching nose.

The whole truth
Uncovering deception applies as well to selection and appraisal interviewing as to security screening. People are just as likely to try to pull the wool over the interviewer's eyes. In a survey of 1500 companies it was found that 71% had encountered serious lying on CVs. The most common lies on CVs were 31% about previous experience, 21% about university qualifications, 19% about salary and 18% about

secondary qualifications (*Experian Survey in the Guardian*, 15th January 2000).

So how does the interviewer manage the situation? It has been suggested (*Bad Lies in Business*) that subtle rewards and punishments should be used when distinguishing between perceived 'truths' and 'lies'. For example, if the interviewee appears to be speaking honestly then:

- the response should be friendly and open, eg the 'palms-up' gesture
- first names should be used
- the interviewer should look directly at, and smile at the interviewee
- personal space can be increased between the two of them by leaning or moving back.

On the other hand, if the interviewee appears to be imparting something less than the truth, then the response can be more confrontational. For example:

- use gestures such as finger pointing
- gaze at the individual for slightly longer than usual or look away
- use the subject's surname rather then first name, or even
- lean forward to decrease personal space.

The aim here is to counter the apparent deception and draw it out into the open.

A word of warning
As a word of warning to the overly zealous – non-verbal

communication provides clues to how people think and feel, not evidence. Just because someone appears nervous or behaves uncharacteristically does not prove wrong-doing.

Body language in security and control

Those who guard, control, observe or investigate, such as the police, security personnel and insolvency practitioners, are tasked with the responsibility of protecting the public. They have a helping function and yet their presence can, under certain circumstances, appear threatening.

For those directly involved in security activities there is, therefore, a need to balance the perception of the **helping** function with that of **control**, particularly if the public are to view their services in a positive light. In recent years, for example, armed police have maintained a presence at some of our major international airports.

It is precisely for this reason that armed officers must be seen to be alert and professional, yet relatively inconspicuous. Were they to act inappropriately – leaning in doorways, chewing gum – they would undoubtedly alarm the very people they were sent to protect.

It is the ability to spot inappropriate, or 'out-of-place' body language in others that enables security personnel to respond quickly to complex situations and to distinguish between those that carry a threat and those that do not. For example, the panic engendered by a mother losing sight of her child in a public place would not be interpreted as threatening, even though the body language of those involved might indicate high levels of anxiety and stress.

During one training course a female airport security officer reported that she had apprehended a woman who was carrying drugs strapped to her body. The woman looked pregnant but, according to the security officer, her suspicions were aroused because the suspect didn't have a 'pregnant face'. Such sensitivity to detail (the language of the body) has much to do with intuition, or having a 'experienced eye for the unexpected'.

Airport security – high stress, low tolerance
In his book *Manwatching*, Desmond Morris found that more verbal and physical aggression is exhibited at airports, railway stations, bus stations and ports than in most other public places. Airports, in particular, are subject to high levels of such **stress-related behaviour**.

But why? According to Morris, it is because travel, and especially air travel, is innately stressful. Just getting to the airport can be a nightmare. Traffic jams, detours, accidents, panic over missing the plane, things left behind ...

The two most common causes of anxiety are:

- Fear of flying
  Morris found that people exhibit ten times as many signs of tension (displacement activities) at airports as at railway stations. Only 8% of the passengers about to board a train showed these signs, but the figure rose to 80% at the check-in desk of a jumbo jet flight.
- Loss of personal space
  Aggressive body language arises when people are forced to wait in queues, are crowded into restrictive spaces, or feel crammed into aeroplane seats.

The notion of 'personal space' is also culturally determined. In the USA and Western Europe, 'one's own space' is said to be anything under an arm's length; in Mediterranean cultures, it is under elbow length, whilst in eastern Europe it is about 'wrist' length.

Given that people of all cultures regularly mix at airports it means that levels of tolerance are bound to differ and clashes to occur. When they do, those in the front line at airports who are responsible for managing the public – immigration, customs and excise, police, security and airline personnel – have to deal with whatever arises while remaining polite, calm and in control.

Recognising tension
Being able to **recognise tension** in others is a first step towards limiting confrontation and alleviating stress. Cabin crew are specially trained to watch for tell-tale signs of tension, particularly amongst fidgeting passengers, which can include:

- repeatedly checking tickets or passports
- rearranging hand-luggage
- dropping things
- constantly making 'vital last minute checks'
- changing position in their seats
- grimacing
- head scratching
- earlobe tugging
- lighting but not smoking cigarettes
- repeatedly breaking matches
- rubbing the back of the neck with the palm of the hand.

When tension cannot be **displaced** in these ways, it begins to flow over in the form of aggression. Sometimes this may be **directed** at inanimate objects like airport furniture or through door slamming. At other times it may be **targeted** at airport staff *verbally* through argument and confrontation, or *non-verbally* in the form of aggressive body language.

Staff who find themselves at the centre of an 'incident' – for example, when a disageement threatens to become physically aggressive – may, quite simply, have been insensitive to the moods and feelings of those they are dealing with. For example; the following can all result in increasing the conflict:

- raising one's voice
- pointing
- rolling one's eyes in frustration, and
- standing too close.

It has been noted that some security staff tend to be involved in more 'incidents' than others and it is often their body language, tone of voice or other mannerisms that make them 'incident prone'; to put it simply they have inadvertantly caused the problem to escalate.

Ambiguous gestures
One of the problems with gestures that people use when they are anxious, angry, frightened or belligerent is that they can mean different things to those of different ethnic or cultural backgrounds. What may be insulting in one country might not be in another, and what might be considered a light-hearted gesture to some, can have serious implications to others.

In Saudi Arabia touching the lower eye lid with the forefinger indicates stupidity, although in other cultures the same gesture implies 'secrecy' or disbelief. Tapping or twisting the forefinger against the temple are also variants of the stupidity gesture, but since in some cultures these imply that you have a screw loose or that your brain is going round and round, it could be that misinterpretation will result in aggressive counter-reaction.

Similarly, the Greek Moutza, in which an open hand is thrust towards another person, meaning 'get lost', means 'stop there' to police and security officers in the UK. Using both hands with the palms held vertically might reduce the risk of misunderstanding.

Another 'get lost!' gesture can cause problems if incorrectly interpreted. This is the 'chin-flick' which occurs when the back of the fingers are swept upward and forward against the underside of the chin. Desmond Morris points out that while this gesture means 'get lost' in France and northern Italy, in southern Italy it means 'no', or 'I do not want any'.

Predicting aggression
There are a number of gestures that exemplify aggressive behaviours which can be useful predictors of potential conflict situations.

- *Shaking the fist* at someone expresses contempt.
- *Hand chop or hand slice* whereby the hand is used like an axe to suggest execution.
- *Prodding with the fingertips* in the direction of another person's eyes.
- *Finger pointing*, less aggressive than prodding, is nevertheless threatening. For those in security who

need to gain someone's attention it is better to use the whole hand to point rather than the forefinger.
- *Staring or 'eyeballing'*, as boxers do before a fight, is designed to intimidate or control a situation.
- *Crowding* or invading someone's personal space is also about control. Standing in close proximity has long been known as a means of exerting pressure on someone (raising stress levels).

It goes without saying that exerting pressure in this way can be interpreted as coercion and such techniques need to be used with sensitivity and care. Fortunately, most threats of aggression do not result in physical violence as most people ultimately prefer to avoid injury.

For those involved in security and crowd management it is well to note the precursors to actual violence, the non-verbal signals that body language betrays. One of the giveaways in this respect is what is known as **adrenalising** – part of the body's fight or flight response when adrenalin is pumped round the system in preparation for action. In such cases, breathing tends to speed up and deepen, sweating occurs, the mouth begins to feel dry and the individual may lick his lips and start swallowing. Face tone turns pale and shivering may begin, symptoms that Desmond Morris describes as 'the cold sweat of fear'.

At the same time that the nervous system is gearing up for action, body posture begins to alter. Squaring up is the body's response to signals of danger. Here, the eyes narrow, the mouth widens, the shoulders are raised and the neck and head are thrust forward. The arms tend to be slightly bent and the fists begin to clench. As the trunk pushes outward, the abdomen contracts and the knees bend to give more 'spring' in defence as well as attack. The whole process makes the body appear more compact and in readiness for combat.

Avoiding confrontation

There are certain basic rules that you need to follow if you are to resolve the confrontational situation to everyone's satisfaction.

- *Be assertive, not confrontational.* Problems are rarely solved through confrontation or argument.
- *Remain calm* and try to ensure that your own body language is neither defensive nor threatening. You need to be seen to be in control.
- *Keep at arm's length.* This allows you to step aside should the individual possibly lunge at you. Never attempt to touch or grab someone who is angry as this will only encourage retaliation. You can always tell if you are getting too close to someone as they will usually step back, lean back or fold their arms in a defensive posture.
- *Don't 'talk down to',* or use gestures that could be interpreted as you implying that the customer is stupid – something more likely to inflame than calm the situation. People are not stupid. They may be difficult, confused, slow, muddled or even disabled in some way, and you especially have to give the benefit of the doubt to someone with sight or hearing limitations.
- *Don't shout* or raise your voice at the customer. Shouting is an aggressive way of communicating and is likely to annoy not only the person you are dealing with, but also those in the immediate vicinity.

- *Avoid pointing* at people. If you want their attention, or you wish to direct them in a certain way, use your whole hand. Try not to point directly at individuals. Even pointing with the thumb, nodding or tossing your head in a certain direction are regarded as a surly gestures and are likely to cause irritation.
- *Don't beckon with the forefinger only* as this is often perceived as demeaning or sarcastic. It is better to roll the fingers towards you with the palms up although in Italy, Spain, South America, Africa and Asia the same gesture is used but with the palms face down. When dealing with children or large groups it is acceptable to use the whole arm to beckon, but this should be done slowly so as to avoid the impression of rushing people. You may have noticed that tour guides and the military raise the whole arm above their heads while rotating the forefingers, meaning 'come around me'.
- *Retain eye contact* with the customer or client to show that you are interested and concerned. Looking down or looking away may be construed as disinterest and cause annoyance.
- *Avoid dissent*, that is, try not to shake your head or wag your finger. If you need to say no it is better to use the whole hands, palms-down gesture whilst at the same time maintaining friendly eye contact.
- *Maintain an upright posture* when sitting, as this appears attentive, professional and lacking in tension. Slouching, hanging legs over chairs, or feet on desks appears disrespectful and leaning back with your hands clasped behind your head and elbows sticking out in front looks 'superior'.
- *Avoid 'picking lint'*. The effect of this gesture is to

indicate that you are not in agreement with someone and that you can't be bothered to argue with them.

- *Show understanding* when the person you are dealing with is getting flustered. Simple gestures, such as patting the palms in a gentle, downward motion combined with comments such as 'I understand your feelings, so let's talk about it', can make a difficult situation less confrontational. The age-old tradition of offering tea or coffee at such times might also not go amiss.

To sum up: an understanding of non-verbal communications can help identify stress and deception and also help to foresee conflict and reduce confrontation.

Are you listening?

Selection, appraisal and counselling

The interview

Every good manager knows that the aim of an interview – whether for selection, appraisal or counselling – is to encourage the interviewee to do most of the talking. This means that the person conducting the interview should be an **active listener** as well as a **questioner**.

As a rule of thumb, managers should aim to ensure that the employee does the talking for about 75% of the time in selection and appraisal, and up to 90% of the time in counselling. Listening, of course, means more than simply hearing the words. Being receptive to the cues that interviewees give through their body language is just as important.

First impressions

In the case of selection interviewing the **first impression** the interviewee and interviewer have of each other often irrationally determines the outcome of the selection process. The interviewer must be aware of such prejudices and the role that body language has on creating these first impressions.

The interviewee is usually nervous and will only tend to talk freely, openly and honestly when he or she begins to feel a rapport with the interviewer. The interviewer has to be careful not to prejudge the interviewee on the basis of these initial signals; the word prejudice, after all, means to prejudge. Research has shown that when we first meet others we automatically make judgements about them; such as personality, intelligence, temperament, working abilities, suitability as a friend or lover and so on.

Sometimes it is **intuition** that informs us, in the sense that we **subconsciously** draw conclusions from **body language cues**. These make us feel secure in our understanding of the person without actually knowing why. Interviewers therefore need to take stock not only of their inevitable prejudices, (particularly relating to social class, gender, ethnic background, dress and appearance), but also of the speculative manner in which initial judgements are formed. There are some simple rules for neutralising first impression bias:

- Be prepared to recognise your own prejudices and make allowances for them.
- Remember that assumptions are not facts and do not constitute evidence.
- Treat each interviewee similarly and try to ask the same questions (so that an objective comparison can be made between candidates).

Getting comfortable

In all three types of interview, getting the interviewee to relax at the very start is important, as people tend to be more open and honest if they feel at ease. So don't begin the process by sitting behind a desk as this tends to create a **physical**, and therefore a **psychological, barrier**. It is often better to sit on low chairs round a coffee table or opposite each other using the corner of a table, as this creates a more relaxed atmosphere.

'There is something about this candidate I do not trust.'

Breaking the ice
The interviewer's initial questions should be very informal
in order to encourage a natural dialogue. You might want
to approach a counselling session obliquely in order to
reduce any possible tension by asking simply and with a
smile: 'Have you done this before? Don't worry, it's easy',
followed by (a palms-up) 'How can I help?'.

However, don't:

- start off with an accusatory tone of voice or remark
- lean too far forward – it's aggressive
- point – also aggressive
- sit back with arms and legs crossed – shows
  defensiveness
- lean back, hands behind head – superiority.

If you appear aggressive, too formal or superior, you will
delay getting to know each other and give the other person
less of a chance to participate effectively. You may even

witness their **physical retreat** as they fold their arms and legs defensively.

Active listening

The manager as active listener should sound interested, smile, nod and maintain a reasonable degree of eye contact to encourage rapport. They should be watching as well as listening, to take on board the other person's body language:

- Cocking the head shows that you are actively listening.
- Nodding the head slowly suggests that you are listening and wish the other person to continue.
- A more rapid nod gives the impression that you agree with what you are hearing.

These are non-verbal forms of encouragement and are essential to maintaining the subject's flow of conversation. It also suggests that you **understand** and that you are **taking in** what is being said. But be careful. While this mode of non-verbal agreement may be appropriate to appraisal and counselling situations, in selection interviewing you may be giving your own views away with the result that the interviewee responds according to what he or she thinks you want to hear.

On the other hand, some managers are so intent upon conveying a 'neutral' or 'professional' approach that they conduct interviews – especially selection – as if they are playing poker; the expressionless 'poker face'. So, remember that if you don't smile, nod or provide other 'paralinguistic' forms of encouragement, your neutral body language may well be self-defeating – your interviewee will stop talking.

Making notes
In selection and appraisal you should be making brief notes. If a table is there you may be tempted to use it to rest your notepad, however, this will cause you to look down and, thereby, break eye contact. Quite often, the interviewee will interpret this as time to stop talking, so it is better to use a clip board so as to maintain the eyeline.

Relaxed posture, easy rapport
If neither of you are relaxed, you will not get the best out of the interview situation. So watch out for defensive postures, such as:

- leaning back
- arms folded, ankles crossed
- tense smile.

Research indicates that unrelaxed postures not only reflect but create tension. Most of us know that smiling makes us feel better, so too does a relaxed posture. In fact it helps us to **open up mentally**. So, awareness of your own body language can actually make you think and feel differently.

There are various ways to encourage relaxation. Having tea or coffee not only sets an informal tone, but also stops the interviewee from adopting a closed or defensive posture – and hence a defensive frame of mind.

When counselling an employee, look for the postures that can tell you whether something is wrong. For example:

- drooping shoulders
- lack of eye contact

- a sullen appearance
- looking down.

These all suggest a negative frame of mind. In such cases, the individual is literally 'feeling down'. Similarly:

- Self-protective 'wrapping', in which the arms are folded in front, may suggest withdrawal, or a need to feel safe.
- Fidgeting and changing position suggests anxiety and nervous tension.

'I'm okay – nothing wrong with me.'

Dealing with sensitive issues in an appraisal
If you need to give people constructive feedback (a better phrase than criticism), being **assertive** but **non-threatening** in such situations is important. There are **four basic stages** that you need to follow if you want to appear sensitive rather than threatening: **introduce, expand, expect** and **close.**

Introduce
As a manager you should attempt to introduce the issue in a **neutral and non-threatening** way, being careful to use the kinds of words and phrases that the other person uses.

Above all, avoid any approach or use of posture and
gestures that might cause the other person to retreat, feel
defensive, or to react in a hostile manner. In a case, say,
where an employee's time-keeping is in question, a blunt
approach will just create defensiveness whereas an assertive
though non-accusatory approach will be more likely to get
the right results.

Expand
Having described the situation in a neutral or non-
threatening way you now wish to expand on why the issue
you are raising is **important**. This requires **empathy** on your
part – being able to 'put yourself in the other person's shoes'.

Here, your tone not only reflects that you understand the
individual's point of view, but that you are also showing
concern for the team.

Expect
Having introduced and expanded on the issues you should
now say what you expect from the individual so there are
no misunderstandings in the future.

Close
Now comes the part where you want to finalise the
discussion. You may wish to point out the **negative
consequences** if things don't improve, however, you may
want to conclude on a **positive, optimistic note.**

You can vary the procedure according to the employee's
response. For example, if he or she is apologetic after the
situation has been introduced or gives an undertaking that
things will improve, then there may be no need to proceed
with the other stages.

Throughout, you need to listen to the tone of voice and speed of delivery and to take note of both verbal and non-verbal signals before responding accordingly. It is this that makes you an active listener.

Maintaining rapport
In all three interview situations the manager's job is not to interrogate the interviewee, but to **facilitate** the communication process.

Having established a rapport, how do you then maintain it? In a sense, 'getting on' with someone involves synchronising one's responses to the other. We all do it, often without realising. The NLP experts, O'Connor and Seymour, have gone as far as to argue that rapport involves matching and mirroring body language and tonality.

This doesn't mean exactly copying another person's behaviour. You can use **cross-over mirroring** – the matching of an arm movement with a small hand movement, or a shift in posture with a corresponding movement of the head. This gives the impression that you are in sympathy with each other.

In a similar way, changes in facial expression, tone of voice and use of the hands can make it equally clear that you are **disengaging** from the conversation. This effectively unlocks you from 'duet' and has been called disengaging from the dance since it breaks the pattern of matching and mirroring.

Rapport can also be maintained by being sensitive to the words the other person uses. If you remember, we explained on Monday how different people might think in different ways **visual**, **auditory** and **kinesthetic**. By using the same kind of language as the other person you soon find that you are, so to speak, **on the same wavelength**.

Touching
One of the more contentious issues to do with maintaining rapport concerns **actual physical contact** or touching. In the UK and USA touching work colleagues, especially subordinates, is far less common than on the European mainland and in some cases is frowned upon. This is a pity because the simple gesture of touching someone to show support, encouragement, agreement or gratitude tends to be received with warmth, thereby reinforcing rapport. Sometimes, it is positively helpful to touch someone, as after difficult appraisal or counselling sessions when reaching out a hand to lightly touch an employee's arm, shoulder or back can only be construed as a **gesture of support**.

Among people of the same sex, a pat on the back – preferably the shoulder blades – by a more senior manager is also likely to be seen as a form of **reward**. Indeed, it can be a highly significant gesture as the expression 'I was touched when she thanked me' indicates.

It has also been observed that people are more likely to touch others when giving information or advice, which suggests that touching is a type of **reinforcement** of what is being said. Similarly we touch each other when asking a favour rather than granting one, or when listening to other people's worries rather than them listening to ours. It's as if we're saying 'We are friends, so can you help me out with ...' , or 'I understand, tell me about it.'

Fact or fiction?

We have talked about uncovering deception in security situations where the concern is deliberate concealment and falsification. In appraisal and counselling you more often find people **in denial** or being 'economical with the truth'; that is, covering up for their weaknesses and failures.

In the selection interview the one thing that the interviewer needs to know for sure is whether the interviewee is telling the truth about qualifications, experience and skills. Asking for documentary evidence and references is a partial way of checking someone's honesty, but face-to-face interviews can help you distinguish fact from fiction.

The astute manager can usually pick up hints of self-deception or denial from observing the interviewee's body language. It is sometimes as if the body is telling a different story from that which the words convey. Take the case of what we call 'uncomfortable truths'.

You come across an issue during the course of discussion that you follow up in order to gain clarity. Instead of the straightforward answer that you expect, the interviewee goes silent. You press further and you get an exaggerated response – a shifting of position, crossed arms, attempts to avert your gaze. When you suggest that the issue is perhaps not quite as clear as was first assumed, the interviewee vehemently denies that the situation occurred, or argues that it cannot be construed in the way that you are describing it. What do you do?

If you press much harder the chances are that you will lose rapport altogether. The point here is whether or not you have found out what you were looking for. In selection and appraisal you would undoubtedly have touched upon a weakness or a concealment of some kind.

In the counselling situation you **encourage** rather than press the individual to open up and, in the process, you may come across a problem, which is **masked** by the reaction. Even if there is an 'uncomfortable truth' involved here, what you don't do is put pressure on the person to talk. Sensitivity to what is going on 'behind the scenes' is all important.

Taking the strain
When people are under too much pressure it tends to show in their moods, body language and ability to cope with everyday tasks. Popularly referred to as **stress**, this much-abused term has come to mean almost anything in occupational life that is to do with being under pressure.

Actually, 'stress' is a **natural state of readiness for action**, rather like the stress you put on a car's suspension under normal load. **Strain**, on the other hand, describes what happens when a person's natural resources **cannot cope** adequately with the demands being made upon them.

For those who have limited control over their working lives, stress is a normal phenomenon. But when it becomes too much and things start to go wrong, more often than not it is because someone in a superior position has failed to identify and deal with the situation.

There are many ways in which strain manifests itself. Usually this is when people who normally cope reasonably well with pressure start to exhibit the body language signs of irritability, anxiety, aggression and tension, or, at the opposite end of the scale, lethargy, apathy and depression.

Very often people who are under strain will convey through their body language that something is wrong. For example, they may:

- become hypersensitive to mild criticism, or even to helpful advice
- display tense postures
- show irritation, such as shrugging the shoulders, 'tutting' or casting their eyes to the ceiling.

On the other hand, if the problems are closer to the surface, they may:

- appear restless
- tremble
- exhibit nervous laughter or incoherent speech.

You may even notice signs of dis-stress, such as:

- sweating
- eye dilation
- increased swallowing due to dryness of the mouth.

Being able to read and understand **pressure signals** is essentially a matter of experience. During interviews it is always worth noting **signs of discomfort** as these may indicate that something is wrong. As we mentioned previously, false yawns, artificial smiles, hand rubbing, picking lint, averting one's eyes and fidgeting, are all common indicators of stressful behaviour.

Body language of strain

To the experienced eye, the body language of strain is not difficult to detect. The slight stoop of the depressed person, the recurring back-ache of the overloaded employee, the hang-dog look of the defeated colleague, the distracted glances of the anxious supervisor, are all indicative of problems that are failing to be identified or alleviated.

The sympathetic touch

It is important to realise that working with people's feelings is a skill that some perform more naturally than others. Learning such skills often requires you to **get in touch** with feelings that are beneath the surface and often come out in posture, gesture and tone of voice.

A common mistake made in these situations is to confuse **advice-giving** with **counselling**. You can be a good listener, you can be empathetic and encouraging, and you can come up with solutions to surface problems, but you may not actually recognise the underlying causes or be able to deal with their unexpected consequences.

If, as a manager, you find that an interview – particularly over disciplinary issues – is turning into a counselling session, you will need to change your approach. This may involve referral to a counsellor. If you do proceed, you will probably find that you are dealing with one or more of the three main causes of emotional turmoil:

Guilt, loss and failure

One of these may be relatively simple to unravel but, in combination, they can pose a considerable problem in terms of management. Sometimes getting to the source of the problem is masked by **anger** on the one hand and **fear** on the other and only sensitive probing will enable you to gain the confidence of the individual in question to talk about how they feel.

It is essential to note the body language of over-expressive, anxious and 'unfulfilled' behaviour:

- the tautness of anger
- the hang-dog look of unhappiness
- the hunched, burdened look
- the listless, apathetic depressed colleague
- the shrunken posture of failure
- the darting eyes of guilt
- the wracked expression of loss
- the hollow-eyed look of fear.

It is equally essential to note the **verbal cues** that people give you – language that expresses physical or psychosomatic ailments. These can sometimes be a guide to stress at work:

- back-ache very often relates to lack of support
- laryngitis to speechlessness
- stomach trouble to 'not being able to stomach' something

- tension headaches to pressure
- breathlessness to fear of performing badly
- blurred vision to panic, or loss of perspective.

In fact many physical conditions that we might never think of in terms of emotions have directly similar parallels.

Once you have gained the **insight** into these issues and the **skills** to deal with them effectively they will become **natural** to you and you will find that people increasingly relax in your company.

Summary

The understanding and awareness of body language gives the manager the clues and insights essential if he or she is to move from mere management to the modern role of coach and facilitator.

Body language provides the manager with a whole new world of insight and understanding. It is like putting on glasses for the first time when you become short sighted – and for those of us who do wear glasses we can truly hear better with our glasses on.

Bibliography

Comer, C, et al, *Bad Lies in Business*, McGraw Hill (1992).

French, J, R & Raven, B, 'The causes of social power', in Cartwright, D & Zander, A, (eds), *Group Dynamics*, Tavistock Publications (1968).

Hay, Julie, *The Sunday Times*, 15/9/96.

Morris, D, *Manwatching*, Grafton Books (1978).

O'Connor, J & Seymour, J, *Training with NLP*, Thorsons (1994).